Other titles in the A Retreat With... *Series:*

A RETREAT WITH POPE JOHN PAUL II

Be Not Afraid

Jack Wintz, O.F.M.

ST. ANTHONY MESSENGER PRESS

Cincinnati, Ohio

Scripture citations are taken from the *New Revised Standard Version Bible*, copyright ©1989 by the Division of Christian Education of the National Council of Churches of Christ in the U.S.A. and used by permission.

Excerpts from *Crossing the Threshold of Hope* by His Holiness Pope John Paul II, translated by Vittorio Messori, copyright ©1994 by Alfred A. Knopf, a division of Random House, Inc. Used by permission of Alfred A. Knopf, a division of Random House, Inc.

Excerpts from John Paul II's *The Pope Speaks to the American Church: John Paul's Homilies, Speeches, and Letters to Catholics in America,* copyright ©1992, are reprinted by permission of HarperCollins Publishers.

Excerpts from John Paul II's "On Social Concern" *(Sollicitudo Rei Socialis), Redemptor Hominis, The Consecrated Life, Dies Domini,* "On The Christian Meaning of Suffering" *(Salvifici doloris),* "Letter to the Elderly," "Message of the Holy Father Pope John Paul II for the First Annual World Day of the Sick," Homily of the Holy Father on the "Day of Pardon" (March 12, 2000), Speech of the Holy Father, Tel Aviv Airport (March 21, 2000), Speech of the Holy Father, Manger Square (March 22, 2000) and Homily of John Paul II at Mass in the Church of the Holy Sepulchre (March 26, 2000), are reprinted by permission of Libreria Editrice Vaticana.

Cover illustration by Steve Erspamer, S.M.
Cover and book design by Mary Alfieri

ISBN 0-86716-420-4

Library of Congress Cataloging-in-Publication Data

Wintz, Jack.
    A retreat with Pope John Paul II : be not afraid / Jack Wintz.
        p. cm. — (A retreat with— series)
    Includes bibliographical references.
    ISBN 0-86716-420-4 (pbk.)
    1. Spiritual retreats—Catholic Church. 2. John Paul II, Pope, 1920-
I. Title. II. Series.
    BX2376.5 .W56 2001
    269'.6—dc21
                                                2001005936

Published by St. Anthony Messenger Press
www.AmericanCatholic.org
Printed in the U.S.A.

DEDICATION

*For my mother
and father*

Contents

Introducing A Retreat With...

Several years ago, Gloria Hutchinson took up the exhortation once given to Thomas Merton: "Keep on writing books that make people love the spiritual life." Through her own writing and that of many gifted others, Gloria brought flesh and format to this retreat series.

It is with a deep appreciation for her foresight that I have assumed the role of series editor. Those of you who have returned to this series again and again will not be jarred by the changes; they are few and subtle. Those of you who are new will find, I hope, that God works to reach us in any manner we will permit, if we but take the time to come aside for a while and wait for the spirit.

The many mentors who have come to life in the pages of this series are not meant to be a conglomeration of quotes by and about them. They are intimate portraits, drawn by authors who know their subject well. But just as our viewing of the *Mona Lisa* tells us more about ourselves than about Leonardo's relationship with his mysterious subject, so the real value in these retreats comes from the minds and hearts of their readers. You are invited to dream and doubt, muse and murmur. If you find a mentor's words compelling, the end of each book has a list of resources to deepen your acquaintance. If you find some of your mentor's ideas challenging, or even disturbing, you can be sure the spirit is at work.

Come aside for a while...

Kathleen Carroll
Series Editor

Getting to Know Our Director

Introducing Pope John Paul II

From his earliest years, the character and spirit of Karol Wojtyla were tested by severe challenges. Like blows from a sculptor's mallet, these tests helped shape him into a prayerful man and a model of heroic faith.

Heroic faith marked his pontificate as he led the Roman Catholic Church toward and across the threshold of the third millennium. Heroic faith, therefore, is our prism for viewing the journey of Karol Wojtyla, better known to us as Pope John Paul II.

In this biographical sketch, we examine first the lived faith of our mentor, and then his faith-filled words and teachings. As Pope John Paul II himself suggests in his *Gift and Mystery*, published on his fiftieth anniversary as a priest, "...people today look to priests for the 'lived word' before they look to them for the 'proclaimed word.'"[1]

Foundations of Faith

Karol Josef Wojtyla (voy-TIH-wah) was born May 18, 1920, in Wadowice, Poland, an industrial town not far from Cracow. At eight years of age he suffered the loss of his mother Emilia Wojtyla who died in 1929 while giving birth to a stillborn child. Just four years later, when Karol was twelve, his much-admired brother Edmund, a physician, died in Cracow of scarlet fever contracted from a patient. Clearly a shadow of grief hung over the young Karol's life.

From early on, however, his inner life was bolstered by a profound faith. His family home, a one-room apartment, stood very close to the parish church. The family prayed together, morning and evening, and young Lolek (to use Karol's nickname) took holy water on entering or leaving the apartment. After his mother's death, his father, a retired army Lieutenant also named Karol, accompanied his son to daily Mass.

In 1930, young Lolek went with his father on a pilgrimage to the monastery of Czestochowa to pray at the shrine of the Black Madonna. The Black Madonna is an important Polish icon. Legend says it was painted by Saint Luke. It dates from at least 1382 and is linked to many miraculous healings.

Throughout his life, Karol Wojtyla has had a great devotion to Mary, the mother of Jesus. While some observers link this to the early and traumatic loss of his mother, others simply attribute it to his strong beliefs as a devout, traditional, Polish Catholic.

During his high school years, Karol showed a great interest and aptitude in poetry and theater, as well as in sports. He played goalkeeper on the soccer team. It is often pointed out that many of his friends and teammates were Jewish.

After graduating from high school in 1938, Karol moved to Cracow with his father and entered Jagiellonian University. There he concentrated on poetry and drama and became active in Studio 38, an experimental theater group.

On September 1, 1939, the Nazis invaded Poland. That morning, as an air attack engulfed the city and kept most citizens off the streets, Karol, in an act of bold faith, went to the cathedral to serve Mass.

Seeking to wipe out Poland's culture and religion, the Nazis soon closed Jagiellonian University. Professors, artists and writers were deported to concentration camps. Priests and nuns were arrested and sent to the camps as well. Karol and other courageous students, nevertheless, continued attending classes secretly through an underground network of university professors.

Meanwhile, Karol's father was plunged further into poverty because the Nazis put a halt to all benefits going to Polish army veterans. The faith of both father and son was seriously tested during this time.

A highly committed and zealous layman named Jan Tyranowski became Karol's spiritual guide and mentor. Tyranowski led a prayer and discussion group in which the future pope took part and was encouraged to lead a life dedicated to God. Through Tyranowski, Karol was introduced to the writings of John of the Cross and Teresa of Avila.

In order to escape deportation after the Nazi invasion, Karol took a laborer's job in a limestone quarry in 1940. Later he was transferred to the Solvay chemical plant, which produced materials for explosives as well as for water filtration. Karol's years as a laborer helped him develop a lifelong respect and solidarity with those who work with their hands.

On February 18, 1941, while taking food to his father's apartment, Karol discovered that his father had died and—worst of all—he had died alone. Karol's father had often expressed his desire that his son find a priestly vocation. His father once told him, "I will not live long and I would like to be certain before I die that you will commit yourself to God's service."[2] It seems that Karol was not yet ready to make that commitment, however; his father died without receiving the assurance for which he had hoped. By the age of twenty, Karol had lost all of his family and had to face the hard truth that he was now completely alone.

The same year, Karol became involved in the Rhapsodic Theater, a banned organization, which put on underground performances of patriotic Polish plays for select audiences. It was important for Karol and his fellow dramatists—in the face of stifling oppression from foreign occupiers—to help keep the cultural values of their nation alive.

Seminarian and Priest

By 1942, Karol had discerned that God was calling him to the priesthood. He became one of the first ten seminarians to study in a secret seminary created by Cardinal Adam Sapieha, archbishop of Cracow. Seminary instruction was clandestine and conducted on a one-on-one basis. Participating in such activity was dangerous: If the Nazis were to discover them, they could face deportation to death camps or immediate execution.

In time, Cardinal Sapieha brought all the seminarians into his residence at the archbishop's palace. In January of 1945, the Nazis left Cracow, and Karol studied for the priesthood with greater confidence and purpose. He was ordained in 1946 on All Saints' Day (November 1) by Cardinal Sapieha.

Shortly after his ordination, Father Karol was sent to Rome to get an advanced degree in theology at the Angelicum University (Pontifical University of St. Thomas Aquinas). His thesis dealt with the notion of faith as found in the life and writings of John of the Cross.

After finishing his studies, Karol returned to Poland in 1949. He took a position as a parish priest in a rural church east of Cracow.

The next year, he was transferred to St. Florian's, an upscale parish in Cracow. Located near Jagiellonian University, St. Florian had a large student community, which Karol served as chaplain. Alongside his pastoral duties, Father Karol found time to write and publish poetry, drama and essays.

He resumed his studies to obtain a second doctoral degree, this time in philosophy. The focus of his doctoral thesis was the ethics of Christianity, using the work of Max Scheler, a German phenomenologist. When the theology department was eliminated in 1954 (Poland was now under Communist rule), Karol followed his instructors to the seminary at Cracow to finish his degree.

It was at this time that he began teaching social ethics at Cracow seminary and also became professor of ethics at the Catholic University of Lublin. He gained a reputation as one of Poland's leading ethical teachers. Aside from his academic pursuits, Father Karol remained popular among university students as a leader of camping, skiing and kayaking trips.

Bishop, Archbishop, Cardinal

In 1958, Father Karol Wojtyla was named auxiliary bishop of Cracow by Pope Pius XII. It was to be a year of remarkable developments for the new bishop. Later in the year, Pope Pius XII died and was succeeded by Pope John XXIII, who soon announced the Second Vatican Council— one of the most significant Church gatherings in history. Bishop Wojtyla attended all four sessions of Vatican II (1962-1965), serving on several important committees. He was gaining notice as a prominent international figure.

During Vatican II in December of 1963, Pope Paul VI named Bishop Wojtyla archbishop of Cracow. The new archbishop—in collaboration with Cardinal Stefan Wyszinski, the primate of Poland—was becoming a leading defender of the Church's rights in its struggle with Poland's repressive Communist regime. In June of 1967, Archbishop Wojtyla was named cardinal.

Accordingly, when Paul VI died on August 6, 1978,

Cardinal Wojtyla was a member of the conclave that chose Paul's successor, Cardinal Albino Luciani. Cardinal Luciani, who took the name Pope John Paul I on August 26, 1978, died unexpectedly a month later (September 28). Cardinal Wojtyla was soon participating in another conclave—this time the one that elected him.

On October 16, 1978, he took the name Pope John Paul II, in honor of his two immediate predecessors. Beating the odds, John Paul II was the first non-Italian pope since Adrian VI, who died in 1523. He was also the first Polish pope in history.

Pope

An evangelizing spirit has marked John Paul's pontificate. With an unflinching faith and total trust in God's love and power, John Paul II has fearlessly followed Christ's command to "Go and make disciples of every nation." He dramatically expanded the global mission of the papacy by embarking on more than ninety pastoral and evangelizing trips outside of Italy—many to developing nations.

On these pilgrimages, John Paul preached and led eucharistic gatherings before enormous crowds. Boldly, he placed his brilliant skills as preacher, stage artist and communicator at the service of the gospel. His personal appeal also won him amazing success with the media (print, radio, television), greatly expanding his outreach to Catholic and non-Catholic alike.

His wide visibility entailed risks, though, as would soon become evident. On May 13, 1981, while John Paul II was riding through St. Peter's Square in a Jeep, greeting the crowd, a Turkish terrorist named Mehmet Ali Agca shot him. Seriously wounded, the pope was rushed to a hospital where he underwent major surgery and was hospitalized for seventy-seven days. In a spirit of reconciliation, the pope later visited Ali Agca in his prison cell.

Many believe that John Paul II played a major role in the collapse of Communism in Eastern Europe and the former U.S.S.R., and furthered the spread of democracy in many places. At the same time, he did not hesitate to speak out against the excesses of capitalism, the growing gap between the rich and the poor, and the exploitation of those who have no voice.

He took his role as teacher and guardian of the faith seriously. He wrote more than fifteen encyclicals and many other documents. His approach to theology and ethics has been careful and conservative. He approved and authorized the *Catechism of the Catholic Church*, published in 1992. Yet, he firmly promoted many of the reforms of Vatican II as well as the Church's social teachings. His firm stance against the death penalty, outspoken defense of human rights, concern for the poor and respect for human life in all its stages demonstrate this.

Pope John Paul II has also shown much interest in promoting ecumenical and interfaith dialogue. In his encyclical *"Ut Unum Sint"* ("That All May Be One") he appeals for the reunion of all Christians. He even asks for advice from other Christian bodies as to how the exercise of papal authority could be changed to facilitate the cause of unity. Having grown up with Jewish friends, he has shown a special interest in improving Catholic-Jewish relations.

In October of 1986, Pope John Paul II invited 150 representatives of a dozen world religions (including Hinduism, Buddhism, Judaism and Islam) and leaders of various Christian churches to Assisi, Italy, for a World Day of Prayer for Peace. This gathering, under the patronage of Saint Francis of Assisi, was one of the great interfaith events of the century.

The Jubilee celebration of the year 2000 was, of course, a high point of the papacy of John Paul II. In this regard, two events are worthy of special notice. First is the special ceremony during a Mass on March 12, 2000, in which the pope asked for God's forgiveness for the past and present sins of Christians. The second is the pope's trip to the Holy Land, from March 20 through March 26 of that year. Among the key places visited by the Holy Father were Bethlehem, Nazareth and Jerusalem's Holy Sepulcher. He also stopped to pray at the Wailing Wall, the holiest site of Judaism, where he left a note asking pardon for sins against the Jewish people.

In a true sense, his visit to Bethlehem on the two-thousandth anniversary of the birth of Christ was the culmination of his pontificate. The pope suggested this during his Mass at Manger Square: "The paths that I have taken lead me to this place and to the mystery it proclaims."[3]

Pope John Paul II's World

As we have seen, a central experience in the life of Pope John Paul II was the Second Vatican Council. He had participated fully in all its sessions and reflected profoundly on its documents. From the beginning of his pontificate, he saw the implementation of teachings of Vatican II as an essential part of his role as shepherd of the universal Church.

In addition, John Paul II was also very aware of his role of leading the Church toward the year 2000 and the Great Jubilee Celebration of the birth of Christ. Surely, he fulfilled the prediction made by his friend and mentor Cardinal Stefan Wyszynski when John Paul II was elected pope: "If the Lord has called you, you must lead the Church into the third millennium."

John Paul II was blessed with an extraordinary

faith in God's power and love within him. He was also endowed with a spirit of deep prayer, a deep love for the Eucharist and the rich traditions of Catholicism. Being the first Polish pope, John Paul brought a special brand of courage, intense faith in Christ, and many other cultural gifts to the papacy and to the universal Church.

Part of our task in this retreat is to take John Paul's great faith and devotion to Christ and apply them to our own lives. Obviously, John Paul was born in a time and place very different from our own. Just as he, under the guidance of the Spirit, placed his unique talents, skills and spiritual vision at the service of the gospel, so must we.

Notes

[1] Pope John Paul II, *Gift and Mystery: On the Fiftieth Anniversary of My Priestly Ordination* (New York: Image, 1999), p. 92.

[2] John Christensen, *Pope John Paul II: The Early Years: An Unhappy Childhood* (CNN.com:2000).

[3] Speech of the Holy Father, Manger Square, Bethlehem, Israel, March 22, 2000.

DAY ONE

'Open Wide the Door to Christ'

Introducing Our Retreat Theme

My alarm radio went off early, as usual, that October morning in 1978. Still half asleep, I was distantly aware of a resonant male voice, ringing with conviction and drama, saying: "Be not afraid." As my drowsiness wore off, I grasped more clearly what the speaker was boldly proclaiming: Jesus Christ is present in human history, and we have nothing to fear.

The voice was that of Pope John Paul II, speaking from St. Peter's Square in Vatican City at the very beginning of his papacy, October 22, 1978. "Brothers and Sisters," the pope proclaimed with vibrant faith, "don't be afraid to welcome Christ and to accept his power."

The central theme of this retreat is: Be not afraid to open the door to Christ. This was surely a central focus of the preaching and writing of our retreat master, Pope John Paul II, and a firm conviction modeled by his own life. In fact, Christ the Redeemer was the focus of the pope's very first encyclical *"Redemptor Hominis"* ("Redeemer of the Human Race"), released in 1979.

Throughout his pontificate, Pope John Paul was keenly aware of the approaching third millennium and the great Jubilee year marking the two-thousandth anniversary of Jesus' Incarnation. "Be not afraid to open the door to Christ" became the watchwords for the approaching celebration.

In Retreat Session One we will draw upon the teaching and example of John Paul II as we delve into our central question: Just who is this Jesus who has entered human history and walks with us powerfully every minute of the day? How do we open ourselves to him without fear? The opening sentence of *"Redemptor Hominis"* states, "The Redeemer of Man, Jesus Christ, is the center of the universe and of history."[1] How can we make Jesus the center of our lives just as Pope John Paul II did?

Opening Prayer

Loving Jesus, John Paul, our brother, has called us to open ourselves to you without the least shred of fear. We can do this because you embody God's overflowing and healing love. You have entered human history, not to condemn us, but to save us and to reveal to us our immense value and dignity. In your warm, saving embrace, Jesus, help us to overcome our fear and discover that you are our loving Redeemer, full of God's power and love, the model for humanity and the key to our meaning as human beings.

RETREAT SESSION ONE

In *Crossing the Threshold of Hope*, Pope John Paul II looked back on that historic moment in 1978 when he first uttered the words "be not afraid" in St. Peter's Square. The pope insisted, however, that *he* was not the primary source of that bold three-word proclamation, which would be repeated often during his pontificate. The words really came, he said, from "The Holy Spirit, the Consoler promised by the Lord Jesus to his disciples."[2]

The pope commented further,

> *Why should we have no fear?* Because man has been redeemed by God. When pronouncing those words... I already knew that my first encyclical and my entire papacy would be tied to the truth of the Redemption. In the Redemption we find the most profound basis for "Be not afraid!": "For God so loved the world that he gave his only Son" (cf. Jn. 3:16)... *The power of Christ's Cross and Resurrection is greater than any evil which man could or should fear.*[3]

Two Meanings of Fear

In discussing this further, the pope explored the different meanings of fear found in the Bible. "The Holy Scriptures," he points out, "contain an insistent exhortation to cultivate the fear of God. We are speaking here of that fear which is a gift of the Holy Spirit."[4] The pope specifically singled out the verse: "The fear of the Lord is the beginning of wisdom."[5]

But the word *fear* in this context, says the pope, needs special understanding, "This fear—the origin of wisdom—has nothing in common with the fear of a slave." The fear we must avoid, as in the phrase "be not afraid," he says, is servile fear—the kind of fear a slave has toward an unloving master. On the other hand, the fear praised in the psalm is what the pope calls "filial fear." Filial fear is like the loving respect or reverence a son or daughter has toward loving parents, which is the opposite of servile fear![6] The wisdom-based fear of God is a sense of wonder and awe that one feels when encountering the majesty and incredible love of God. This fear is really an appreciation of the wondrous mystery that is God.

We may also find it helpful to look at fear in terms of the fear of loss. It is wise to appraise and rank the things we value—or put conversely, the things we most fear to lose. Many of us fear losing our money, titles, popularity or health more than we fear losing God—the actual source of all our riches. The first principle of wisdom is to put God first. Perhaps this helps us see a bit more clearly how the fear of God is the beginning of wisdom.

For where our treasure is, there is where our heart will be, says Jesus.[7] We need to imitate the man in Jesus' parable who finds a treasure buried in a field and goes out and sells all he has to buy that field.[8] The treasure, of course, is God. The person who puts God before all else truly possesses a proper fear of God, that is, a true reverence and appreciation of the one who created all things. We must have a fear that is something like the care with which a wise person holds a precious jewel or a glass of rare wine. It is a keen sense of the value of something.

"Every sign of servile fear vanishes before the awesome power of the all-powerful and all-present One. Its place is taken by filial concern."[9] This filial concern, explains the pope, understands that God's plan for us is good.

Jesus: Model for Understanding our Humanity

All human beings wrestle with questions like: Who am I? Why am I here on earth? What is meaning of my life? What is my role in life? What is my value or destiny as a human being? To answer these questions, we look to Jesus as the key.

"'Christ...fully reveals man to himself and brings to light his most high calling,'"[10] states John Paul II, quoting the Second Vatican Council. "In Christ and through Christ," he continues, "human persons have acquired full awareness of their dignity, of the heights to which they are raised, of the surpassing worth of their humanity, and of the meaning of their existence."[11]

In June 1979, during his first trip to Poland as pope, John Paul II made an incredibly bold statement that hammered this point home. In the center of Warsaw's Victory Square, the Polish pope said words that gave heart to the Catholic faithful while sending signals of alarm to the Communist Party leaders: "To Poland, the Church brought Christ, the key to understanding the great and fundamental reality that is man."[12] And, because Christ is such a great model for understanding our humanity, "Christ cannot be excluded from human history in any part of the globe, from any latitude or longitude of the earth. Excluding Christ from human history is a sin against humanity."[13]

Convinced that a loving Christ fully reveals to us our meaning as human beings, we embrace, all the more fervently, the pope's plea for this first day of retreat "to open wide the door to Christ."

For Reflection

- *When have you been open to the power of Christ? How do you invite Jesus into your life?*

- *What is your attitude of fear toward God? How does your attitude change in difficult times?*

- *Jesus said, "I stand at the door and knock. If anyone hears my voice and opens to me, I will enter and have dinner with him and he with me." How do you respond to this invitation?*

Closing Prayer

Oh Jesus Lord, risen from the dead and no longer under death's power, we hear you knocking at the doors of our hearts. Help us open our hearts to your immense love—a powerful love which drives out all fear. Be with us during this time of retreat and during every day of our lives. Amen.

Notes

[1] *"Redemptor Hominis,"* #1

[2] Pope John Paul II, *Crossing the Threshold of Hope,* ed., Vittorio Messori (New York: Knopf, 1994), p. 219.

[3] *Crossing the Threshold of Hope,* p. 219.

[4] Isaiah 11:2.

[5] Psalm 110:10.

[6] *Crossing the Threshold of Hope,* p. 226.

[7] See Matthew 6:21.

[8] See Matthew 13:44.

[9] *Crossing the Threshold of Hope,* p. 226.

[10] *"Redemptor Hominis,"* #8.

[11] Adapted from *"Redemptor Hominis,"* #11.

[12] Quoted by Carl Bernstein and Marco Politi in *His Holiness: John Paul II and the History of our Time* (New York: Viking Penguin Books, 1997), p. 6.

[13] Bernstein, p. 6.

DAY TWO
Prayer: Taking Time to Listen

Coming Together in the Spirit

In the summer of 1958, Father Karol Wojtyla had to interrupt his vacation at the Mazurian Lakes, where he had been taking some retreat days with a group of young people. He received a message instructing him to go to Warsaw and appear at the residence of the archbishop, who was then Cardinal Stefan Wyszinski, primate of Poland. When Father Karol arrived, Cardinal Wyszinski presented the thirty-eight-year-old priest with a letter from Pope Pius XII appointing him auxiliary bishop of Cracow.

Father Karol calmly assured the cardinal of his willingness to accept the appointment and left. He went directly to the convent of the Grey Ursuline Sisters and asked to spend some time in the chapel. He walked to the front of the chapel and fell to his knees in the first pew.

Two or three hours went by. Father Karol knelt there silently, head in his hands. One of the nuns asked if he would like to eat. He declined. A few more hours passed. Father Karol continued to pray in silence. He went without food the entire evening and spent eight continuous hours in prayer.

We do not know the specific contents of Father Karol's prayer during those eight hours or what went on between

God and the bishop-elect in the secret center of his heart. But the dramatic incident speaks volumes about the importance, for Karol Wojtyla, of taking time to listen to God in prayer. It conveyed the intensity of his faith and his keen awareness that it is God's power and love—and not primarily his own—that must guide his life and ministry.

This reverent act of stepping aside from the activity of the day to commune with God and contemplate the purpose of his life is a trademark of Pope John Paul II, our retreat director. It is a practice worthy of imitation.

Most of us are aware—at least through the media— of the pope's busy schedule, especially hectic during his pilgrimages to destinations around the world. Still, he maintains his custom of snatching moments of private time to quiet his heart and tap the life of the Spirit within. This was dramatized, for example, during his celebrated visit to the Holy Land during the great Jubilee Year, celebrating the two-thousandth anniversary of the birth of Christ.

Even *The New York Times* did not fail to see and report the pope's practice of setting aside precious moments to listen to the voice of Christ and contemplate the sacred places he was visiting and the profound mysteries they represented.

Bethlehem represents one such mystery of paramount importance. This is how *The New York Times* described the pope's visit there:

> After the Mass [at Manger Square, Bethlehem, March 22], the pope visited the Grotto of the Nativity, kneeling in the cavern in which tradition says Jesus was born, and prayed in solitary silence for more than fifteen minutes.[1]

No doubt, the pope's taking time for private meditation on this solemn occasion made the crowds and dignitaries more than a little nervous and anxious to get on with the schedule. Yet, John Paul II, seeing the importance of this sacred place, felt that he must honor the great mystery of the Incarnation with a lengthy period of prayerful silence.

Two days later, on March 25, the pope paused for a similar period of silent meditation during his visit to Nazareth on the feast of the Annunciation. While those attending the pope waited, John Paul II knelt in silent prayer for ten full minutes in the small Shrine of the Annunciation—the site where Christians believe the angel Gabriel told Mary she would become the mother of Jesus. Again, John Paul saw the need to show this kind of reverence at this sacred place where the Word became flesh two thousand years ago in the womb of a virgin.

In reporting both of these instances, *The New York Times* and other newspapers around the world took care also to run photos showing the pope in private prayer. Devoting space to these photos suggests that even so-called secular journalists sensed the spiritual drama of these gestures. They become reminders for all people to recognize the need to respond reverently to the mystery and presence of God in our world.

Opening Prayer

Loving God, you are always present to us even during our busy activities. As Saint Paul says, "God is not far from any one of us. For 'In him we live and move and have our being'...."[2] We ask you, gracious God, to help us to become more aware of the gift of your presence. Keep us from getting so caught up in our activities—or in our rush to accomplish things—that we lose sight of the immensity of your love and care for us. Help us to learn from the example of Jesus and your servant John Paul II

how important it is to set aside times of silence so that
we can really listen to your guiding voice—and let the
wonder of your presence and love sink in. Amen.

Retreat Session Two

Monks, nuns and members of religious orders,
the Church teaches, have a special call to prayer and
contemplation. When Jesus gathered his first band of
disciples, he was creating this kind of spiritual community.
At the same time, we know the call to prayer is not
restricted to religious communities. All God's people are
offered the gift of contemplation and the invitation to be
united with God in prayer. It is everyone's most sacred
call—a call God places in our hearts.

Pope John Paul II singles out Jesus' transfiguration as
an event that sheds wonderful light on our call to feed the
contemplative hunger within us. John Paul invites us "to
fix our gaze on Christ's radiant face in the mystery of the
Transfiguration."

In the Gospel descriptions of the transfiguration,
we find many elements of contemplative prayer. In one
dramatic instance, we see Jesus inviting Peter, James
and John to withdraw with him from the busy plain of
everyday life and come to a place apart—to a high
mountaintop.

Suddenly the apostles see the humanity of Jesus so
united to God that the divine glory shines through him.
We know from other prayerful moments in Christ's life
that he often needed to go to some deserted place to unite
himself with God in intimate prayer, to surrender himself
to the life of God within him. In prayer, he would make
himself transparent to God, so to speak, and let God's

light shine through him. Here on the mountaintop, God fully revealed his glory through the humanity of Christ, so much so that "his face shone like the sun, and his clothes became dazzling white."[3]

For the three apostles, this was an overwhelming contemplative experience. With their eyes fixed on God's glory in Jesus, they were caught up into this ecstatic experience. They were totally drawn out of themselves and into the glorious cloud of God's presence—and attuned, as well, to the Divine utterance coming from the cloud: "This is my Son, the Beloved; with him I am well pleased; listen to him!"[4]

Jesus is the revealed and glorious face of God. If, in faith, we do take time to truly listen to and contemplate Jesus, the Word of God, and let his radiant face appear, the vision of the transfigured Christ will comfort us in times of trial and challenge.

In the words of Pope John Paul II,

> The Transfiguration is not only the revelation of Christ's glory but also a preparation for facing Christ's Cross. It involves both "going up the mountain" and "coming down the mountain." The disciples who have enjoyed this intimacy with the Master, surrounded for a moment by the splendor of the Trinitarian life..., are immediately brought back to daily reality, where they see "Jesus only," in the lowliness of his human nature, and are invited to return to the valley, to share with him the toil of God's plan and to set off courageously on the way of the Cross....[5]

"This mystery," the pope adds, "is constantly relived by the Church, the people on its way to the eschatological encounter with its Lord. Like the three chosen disciples, the Church contemplates the transfigured face of Christ in order to be confirmed in faith and to avoid being dismayed at this disfigured face on the Cross."[6]

In John Paul II's 1994 best-selling book *Crossing the Threshold of Hope*, we find other helpful insights on prayer. The book is written in question-and-answer format, with questions posed by Italian journalist Vittoria Messori. The pope's responses to questions on prayer are contained in two of the book's early chapters.

In the first of those chapters, Messori asks the pope to share what is in his heart and explain how one can best engage in prayer and dialogue with Christ. "Perhaps it is worth starting with Saint Paul's Letter to the Romans," the pope replies. "The apostle comes to the heart of the matter when he writes: *'The Spirit too comes to the aid of our weakness;* for we do not know how to pray as we ought, but the Spirit himself intercedes with inexpressible groanings.'(cf. Rom 8:26)"[7]

John Paul explains that prayer "is commonly held to be a conversation. In a conversation there are always an 'I' and a 'thou' or 'you.' In this case, the 'Thou' is with a capital T. If at first the 'I' seems to be the most important element in prayer, prayer teaches that the situation is actually different. *The 'Thou' is more important, because our prayer begins with God*."[8] This is what Saint Paul was trying to tell us, the pope explains, in the passage from his Letter to the Romans.

The one who takes the lead role in this prayer or conversation is God.

> *In prayer, then, the true protagonist is God.* The protagonist is *Christ*.... The protagonist is the *Holy Spirit*, who "comes to the aid of our weakness." We begin to pray, believing that it is our own initiative that compels us to do so. Instead, we learn that it is always God's initiative within us, just as Saint Paul has written.[9]

John Paul reinforces his point near the end of the chapter

when he says in brief summary: "Man achieves *the fullness of prayer* not when he expresses himself, but *when he lets God be most fully present in prayer.*"[10]

We conclude Retreat Session Two with a final reflection on prayer from John Paul:

> *Prayer is a search for God,* but it is also *a revelation of God.* Through prayer, God reveals Himself as Creator and Father, as Redeemer and Savior, as the Spirit who "scrutinizes everything, even the depths of God" (I Cor 2:10),...*Through prayer God reveals Himself above all as Mercy*—that is, Love that goes out to those who are suffering, Love that sustains, uplifts, and invites us to trust. A person who prays professes such a truth and in a certain sense makes God, who is *merciful* Love, present in the world.[11]

Pope John Paul II has been for the world a great model of prayer. As we have seen, the pope has taught us—first by his lived example and then by words—that prayer means taking time to listen to God and to drink in the revelation of God's abundant mercy and love.

For Reflection

- *Think of some times in your life when you had to make crucial decisions. Did you make more time for prayer? If not, do you regret your choice?*

- *When do you listen for the voice of God? Do you take reflective moments each morning when you awake? Do you give thanks and praise at meal times? While driving in the car? During breaks in your schedule?*

- *Sometimes we forget that the Sunday Eucharist is a most vital form of prayer. John Paul II has said, "Sunday... is a celebration of the living presence of the Risen Lord in the midst of his own people.... All the faithful should be convinced that they cannot live their faith or share fully in the life of the Christian community unless they take part regularly in the Sunday Eucharistic assembly."*[12] *Are you convinced of the importance of attending Sunday Mass? Do you follow through on your conviction?*

- *Belief in the Communion of the Saints and intercessory prayer enriches the Catholic Tradition. How does it enrich your prayer life?*

Closing Prayer

In your goodness, Lord Jesus Christ, take our faith to a new level so that our prayer—our capacity to commune with you—may itself rise to a new level. The example of John Paul II has taught us that, in the intimate conversation known as prayer, your role and initiative are more crucial than our own. Help us, Jesus, to surrender more to your power and love and the impulses of your spirit that we may serve you on a new, more courageous level. We ask this in your holy name. Amen.

Notes

[1] Alessandra Stanley, "The Pope in the Holy Land: The Overview; Pope, at a Camp, Deplores Plight of Palestinians," *The New York Times*, March 23, 2000.

[2] See Acts 17:27-28.

[3] Matthew 17:2.

[4] Matthew 17:5.

[5] *The Consecrated Life*, #14.

[6] *The Consecrated Life*, #15.

[7] *Crossing the Threshold of Hope*, p. 16.

[8] *Crossing the Threshold of Hope,* p. 16.
[9] *Crossing the Threshold of Hope,* p. 17.
[10] *Crossing the Threshold of Hope,* p. 18.
[11] *Crossing the Threshold of Hope,* pp. 25-26.
[12] *"Dies Domini,"* #31, 81.

DAY THREE
A Message for America

Coming Together in the Spirit

In early October 1979, John Paul II made his first pastoral visit as pope to the United States. For seven days, he gave us a great model for communicating the Good News to our society. He was a messenger of joy, good humor and respect for all. He made us feel good about our identity as human beings, as Americans and as Catholics.

> One image continues to glow in my memory: the image of a happy man who passed his happiness on to others.
>
> Deeply affirmed himself, he affirmed others with his love and steady smile. He sparked celebration and joy wherever he went, and crowds spontaneously broke into songs and laughter whenever he came near. Unexpected humor flowed from him, very comfortably, even on the most solemn occasions....
>
> He did not come across as a negative, hand-wringing moralist because his central message was always positive: the good news of God's love for every human being without distinction. By embracing this truth in his own person, the pope seemed to make millions understand—perhaps for the first time—that the good news is actually good.[1]

It was gray and cloudy when the pope landed at Boston's

Logan International Airport. An enormous crowd had already assembled on Boston Common, the large park near the center of Boston where Pope John Paul II would celebrate a late afternoon Mass. While the pope's motorcade was en route from the airport, the immense crowd waiting anxiously on the common.

> Excitement was mounting all over the park and it was beginning to rain. I heard the distant roar of the police motorcycles leading the motorcade. Enthusiasm shot through the crowd like electricity. Some sections of the crowd could already see the pope and were cheering wildly.
>
> The whirling sound of a helicopter drew my eyes up through the rain into the skies. The police helicopter was apparently hovering over the pope's car.... The pope finally appeared waving and smiling.... "I want to greet all Americans without distinction," he told the jubilant umbrella-dotted crowd. "I want to tell you that the pope is your friend and a servant of your humanity."
>
> The roar of the crowd indicated that Americans would certainly regard him in the friendliest way possible. Warmed by John Paul II's affirming voice, his genuine esteem for all, and his humorous comment that America is beautiful, "even when it's raining," the Boston crowd seemed even to like the rain![2]

During this visit, so often marked by joy and goodwill, one saw in the pope's style of evangelization traces of Vatican II. The documents of the Second Vatican Council suggest a holistic view of our evangelizing mission as Christians. Evangelization today is concerned not only with the "saving of souls" but with the total well-being— body and soul—of all human beings.

Vatican II's celebrated document, "The Church in the Modern World," begins with the concerns of all humanity: "The joy and hope, the grief and anguish of the people of our time, especially of those who are poor or afflicted...are the joy and hope, the grief and anguish of the followers of Christ as well. Nothing that is genuinely human fails to find an echo in their hearts."[3] John Paul was clearly in tune with such sentiments when he proclaimed at Boston Common the already quoted greeting: "The pope is your friend and the servant of your humanity."

Respecting and affirming what is good in a nation's unique history and culture is an important quality of the true evangelist today. Pope John Paul conveyed this kind of respect toward the United States in his homily on the Boston Common:

> On this first day of my visit, I wish to express my esteem and love for America itself, for the experience that began two centuries ago and that carries the name "United States of America"; for the past achievements of this land and for its dedication to a more just and human future; for the generosity with which this country has offered shelter, freedom and a chance for betterment to all who come to its shores; and for the human solidarity that impels you to collaborate with all other nations so that freedom may be safeguarded and full human advancement made possible. I greet you, America the Beautiful.[4]

Opening Prayer

Gracious God and Creator of all, help us to embrace and take pride in the goodness of our heritage as a people, while correcting our failures as well. Help us to become more joyful communicators of the gospel and of the good news of God's love for all. In the spirit of the Second Vatican Council, lead us to show concern for the total well-being of all our sisters and brothers. May the

Holy Spirit guide us to be generous in building up our society so that no one's genuine needs go unmet. Like Jesus, may we come to serve, not to be served. Amen.

Retreat Session Three

Everywhere he went during his visit to the United States, Pope John Paul II showed warm and genuine respect for the history and culture of the United States. He could comfortably do this perhaps because he was a person who, without apology, took great pride in his own culture and history—and could therefore encourage the same for every other nation he visited.

He demonstrated his genuine love for his Polish heritage with special drama more than fifty years ago— on the day of his first Mass as a priest, November 2, 1946—the day after his ordination by Cardinal Sapieha. The place he chose for his first Mass celebration was the crypt of Saint Leonard under Cracow's Wawel Cathedral. The cathedral and its crypt are rich in Polish history. The kings of Poland were crowned and buried there. By having his first Mass there, the pope said, "I wanted to express my spiritual bond with the history of Poland, a history symbolized by the hill of Wawel."[5]

By unabashedly embracing his own national heritage, John Paul helps us to do the same. His action suggests that we do not receive God's love and care as disembodied souls or as abstractions, but as distinct human individuals fashioned by a unique personal and cultural history. Pope John Paul II wanted to take this approach with every human being he met. He sought to love and embrace each person as a unique human being who developed from a precise personal history.

In a sense, John Paul's love for youth was a part of this picture—a part of his respectful attitude for human beings of all classes. The world of youth, of course, is a unique culture in many ways. Throughout his ministry as priest, bishop and pope, John Paul II has always taken the culture of youth seriously and given it special respect and attention.

The World Youth Days he sponsored with great success in cities around the globe have demonstrated this. The World Youth Day held in Rome during the Great Jubilee Year 2000, for example, drew two million young people. For John Paul, the notion that youth are the hope of the future is not just an empty slogan, but a profound reality that deserves our greatest attention.

During John Paul's homily on Boston Common, he was careful to include a special message for American youth. "Again and again," he said, "I find in young people the joy and enthusiasm of life, a searching for truth and for the deeper meaning of the existence that unfolds before them in all its attraction and potential. Tonight I want to repeat what I keep telling youth: You are the future of the world, and 'the day of tomorrow belongs to you.'"[6]

Nor did the pope try to shield his audience from the hard messages of the gospel. He believed in their largeness of soul and their ability to handle the challenges Jesus sets before them. Therefore, at Boston Common, John Paul laid it before them straight:

> I want to remind you of the encounters that Jesus himself had with the youth of his day. The Gospels preserve for us a striking conversation Jesus had with a young man.
>
> We read there that the young man put to Christ one of the fundamental questions that youth everywhere ask: "What must I do...?"(Mk. 10:17),

and he received a precise and penetrating answer ["Sell what you have and give to the poor"]. "Then, Jesus looked at him with love and told him... Come and follow me" (Mk. 10:21). But see what happens: the young man, who had shown such interest in the fundamental question, "went away sad, for he had many possessions" (Mk. 10:22). Yes, he went away, and—as can be deduced from the context—he refused to accept the call of Christ....[7]

To each one of you I say therefore: heed the call of Christ when you hear him saying to you: "Follow me! Walk in my path! Stand by my side! Remain in my love!" There is a choice to be made: a choice for Christ and his way of life and his commandment of love.[8]

Two days later, October 3, 1979, Pope John Paul was again talking to youth, this time at New York's Madison Square Garden. His words, on this occasion, touched on the great theme we addressed in Retreat Session One, namely, that in Christ we all find the key to our meaning as human beings. Jesus is the model and blueprint of the fully developed human being. Jesus is the answer to the question: What is my true meaning, my true role, as a human being? In the pope's own words:

Dear young people...I invite you today to look to Christ.

When you wonder about the mystery of yourself, look to Christ who gives you the meaning of life.

When you wonder what it means to be a mature person, look to Christ who is the fullness of humanity.

And when you wonder about your role in the future of the world and of the United States, look to Christ. Only in Christ will you fulfill your potential as an American citizen and as a citizen of the world community.[9]

Later the same day, the pope came to give a major address
to a large crowd at Battery Park on the southern tip of
Manhattan. It was raining heavily upon the large crowd
awaiting the pope's arrival. Amazingly, the drenching
rain stopped just as the pope's motorcade arrived.

The Statue of Liberty stood in the distance across
the bay. This was important because the pope was about
to make good use of this great American emblem. In his
various trips, Pope John Paul II has shown a genius for
using national symbols to help each nation see its best
ideals and to strive to fulfill them. He did this especially
well on this occasion:

> Dear friends,…my visit to your city would not be
> complete without coming to Battery Park, without
> seeing Ellis Island and the Statue of Liberty in the
> distance. Every nation has its historical symbols.
> They may be shrines or statues or documents; but
> their significance lies in the truths they represent to
> the citizens of a nation and in the image they convey
> to other nations. Such a symbol in the United States
> is the Statue of Liberty. This is an impressive symbol
> of what the United States has stood for from the
> beginning of its history; this is a symbol of freedom.
> It reflects the immigrant history of the United
> States, for it was freedom that millions of human
> beings were looking for on these shores. And it
> was freedom that the young republic offered in
> compassion. On this spot, I wish to pay homage
> to this noble trait of America and its people: its
> desire to be free, its determination to preserve
> freedom, and its willingness to share this freedom
> with others. May the ideal of liberty, of freedom,
> remain a moving force for your nation and for all
> the nations of the world….[10]

And though the pope had praise for American ideals, he
did not shrink from confronting his listeners about the

failures of the rich and the comfortable. He had done this, for example, the previous day at Yankee Stadium. Using the gospel image of the destitute Lazarus starving outside the rich man's gate, the pope spoke out against those who would hoard their wealth and fail to extend a helping hand to those less fortunate. "Do not leave to the poor the crumbs of your feast,"[11] he said.

The next day, Pope John Paul II was in Chicago. Among his activities, he presided at an outdoor Mass at Five Holy Martyrs Church in the heart of the Polish community in Chicago's southwest side. It was a special opportunity to share his faith with his fellow Poles.

Many in the crowd of 200,000 wore traditional Polish dress and the entire liturgy, including the homily, was in Polish. The pope's warm and sometimes humorous comments drew affectionate laughter, as when he referred to reports that the number of Poles in this country had swollen suddenly when he took office—a reference to the jest going about that many Poles rushed to embrace their heritage publicly when their compatriot was elected to the Chair of Peter.

The pope spent the next two days, October 6 and 7, in Washington, D.C. A highlight there was his visit to the White House—making him the first pope ever to do so— and a meeting with President Jimmy Carter on the White House lawn.

His final appearance was on the Washington Mall, midway between the Capitol and the Washington Monument. There he reminded the country of the beauty and dignity of human life: "All human life, from the moment of conception and through all its subsequent stages is sacred, because human life is created in the image and likeness of God."[12]

For Reflection

- How do you measure up to the pope's example of a good evangelist? Does your lifestyle accurately reflect your faith?

- How do you "serve the humanity" of those with whom you come in contact? How do you show concern for the total well-being of those you meet?

- How do you embrace your historical and cultural values? How do you show respect for the heritage of others?

- Are you confident in the goodness and the potential of all, especially young people? How do you express this?

Closing Prayer

Loving God, we thank you for the blessings we have received as a nation. Help us to live out the lofty ideals for which we stand. Help us to have greater confidence in our own goodness as human beings created in your image. Strengthened by your healing love and respect for us, may we show greater compassion to those in need. May we also show love and respect for each person in their unique personal and cultural identity. In imitation of Christ, may we be friends and servants of each other's human development, as together we strive toward the full stature of Christ, in whose name we pray. Amen.

Notes

[1] Jack Wintz, "The Pope in America: Memories to Cherish," *St. Anthony Messenger*, December 1979, p. 25.

[2] "The Pope in America: Memories to Cherish," p. 26.

[3] Adapted from "Pastoral Constitution on the Church in the Modern World" ("*Gaudium et Spes*"), #1, Austin Flannery, O.P., ed. *Vatican Council II: The Conciliar and Post Conciliar Documents*, Vol. 1 (Northport, N.Y.: Costello Publishing Co., 1987), p. 903.

[4] *The Pope Speaks to the American Church: John Paul's Homilies, Speeches, and Letters to Catholics in America* (San Francisco: HarperSanFrancisco, 1992), p. 7.

[5] Pope John Paul II, *Gift and Mystery: On the Fiftieth Anniversary of My Priestly Ordination* (New York: Image, 1999), p 47.

[6] *The Pope Speaks to the American Church*, p. 7.

[7] *The Pope Speaks to the American Church*, p. 7.

[8] *The Pope Speaks to the American Church*, p. 8.

[9] *The Pope Speaks to the American Church*, p. 38.

[10] *The Pope Speaks to the American Church*, p. 39.

[11] Homily at Yankee Stadium, October 2.

[12] "The Pope in America: Memories to Cherish," p. 31.

DAY FOUR
Setting Humanity Free

Coming Together in the Spirit

As we move to Day Four of our retreat, we jump ahead almost twenty years—to January 21, 1998. Pope John Paul II is in Havana, Cuba, on another of his pastoral visits. He has just arrived at the Havana airport and has been greeted by President Fidel Castro. Although the pope's main purpose in coming to this island nation is to encourage the Cuban Church in its Catholic and Christian faith, a significant part of his message deals with human freedom.

John Paul stands only a few yards away from President Castro, whose one-man rule has restricted political and religious freedom in Cuba. But the pope is without fear. Included in his airport address is a bold statement bristling with powerful implications for those sitting next to radios and TVs across Cuba: "You are and must be the principal agents of your own personal and national history."[1] In other words, you are human beings who are meant to be free and to use your freedom to pursue your God-given destinies.

Also, near the end of his address, John Paul conveys his "prayer that this land [Cuba] may offer everyone a climate of freedom, mutual trust, social justice and lasting peace."[2]

And again, on the final day of his highly successful

visit to Cuba, January 25, 1998, the pope returned to the theme of freedom. This happened during his final Mass at Havana's huge Plaza de la Revolucion, the same place where Fidel Castro had made many speeches in praise of the revolution he led in 1959. President Castro was present during this Mass.

Before an immense crowd, estimated by some as close to a million, Pope John Paul II hammered away at his message of freedom: "The state...should encourage a harmonious social climate and a suitable legislation which enables every person and every religious confession to live their faith freely...."[3] Whenever the pope mentioned the notion of freedom, many—including seminarians, priests and religious—jumped to their feet and shouted approval. It was reported that the pope's homily was interrupted twenty-eight times with shouts of "*¡Libertad! ¡Libertad!*" ("Freedom! Freedom!"). The pope insisted, "The attainment of freedom in responsibility is a duty which no one can shirk." He continued:

> For Christians, the freedom of the children of
> God is not only a gift and a task but its attainment
> also involves an invaluable witness and a genuine
> contribution to the journey toward the liberation
> of the whole human race. This liberation cannot be
> reduced to its social and political aspects, but rather
> reaches its fullness in the exercise of freedom of
> conscience, the basis and foundation of all human
> rights.[4]

In these words, the pope makes clear that part of the Church's mission is the "liberation of the whole human race." Even though the Church has cautioned against some forms of liberation theology—those associated with certain unacceptable aspects of Marxism—it is clear that John Paul II is committed to the kind of liberation taught by Christ through word and example.

One can easily observe in Christ's own ministry his desire to set human beings free—to liberate and heal them from everything that hinders their full development as men and women created in the image of God. Indeed, Christ, quoting Isaiah, described his own mission in terms of liberating the poor and the oppressed:

> The Spirit of the Lord is upon me,
> because he has anointed me
> to bring good news to the poor.
> He has sent me to proclaim release
>   to the captives
> and recovery of sight to the blind,
> to let the oppressed go free...[5]

The title we have chosen for this day of our retreat is "Setting Humanity Free." We could have also entitled it "Struggling for Full Human Development," for the two ideas go hand in hand. Human beings are brought to full development by being set free from the obstacles to that development.

Saint Irenaeus put it yet another way when he said, the glory of God is the human person fully alive. What the pope tries to teach us today is how we, as individuals and as the whole human family, are meant to strive—with God's help—for fuller development, fuller freedom and fullness of life.

Opening Prayer

Loving God, give us the gift of true freedom. Help us to become fully alive as your daughters and sons. We know that this is your wish for us and, indeed, the mission of Jesus. Help us to be joyful instruments of your liberation—and of your plan to set the human family free of everything that obstructs their full development and happiness as your children. We ask this in Jesus' name. Amen.

RETREAT SESSION FOUR

There is a perspective among some people, even among some religious people, that the Church should stay out of politics and the struggle for justice and human development. Instead, these people say, the Church should simply concentrate on prayer and the saving of souls. As for those suffering oppression or injustice, well, according to this perspective, they should just be patient and wait for their reward in the next life where they will be set free of their misery.

Our retreat director, Pope John Paul II is flatly opposed to this position, as is demonstrated in the following story. In 1987, the pope was talking with reporters on a flight to Chile. He was on his way to make a pastoral visit to that South American nation during the military dictatorship of Augusto Pinochet. Pinochet and his government had often attacked the Church for its defense of human rights and its involvement in social reform. In Pinochet's view, the Church should stick to prayer and the sacraments and stay out of politics.

The pope told the reporters that he was against this view. He said that those who say, "Stay in the sacristy and do nothing else!" are wrong. He asserted, moreover, that the Chilean Church should speak out for human rights and support the transition to a more democratic society. Indeed, two days later, the pope told the bishops of Chile: "Never hesitate to defend always...the legitimate rights of the person, created in the image and likeness of God. Proclaim your preferential love for the poor...."[6]

The pope has written at length on the subject of human development and liberation. His encyclical letter "On Social Concern" is a good example of the pope's thinking on this subject. "On Social Concern" was published in 1987 on the twentieth anniversary of Pope Paul VI's landmark encyclical "The Development of Peoples," and contained five key points:

Our concern should be global, as well as local. We belong to a human family that is global, and our outlook, says the pope, must be "ruled by...concern for the common good of all humanity, or by concern for the 'spiritual and human development of all' instead of by the quest for individual profit..."[7]

We need to recognize our growing interdependence and the need for collaboration on all sides. Pope John Paul points out that when it comes to full human development, "either all the nations of the world participate, or it will not be true development."[8]

"Today..." the pope adds, "people are realizing that they are linked together by a common destiny, which is to be constructed together, if catastrophe for all is to be avoided."[9]

We must carry on despite difficulties. As John Paul puts it, "Anyone wishing to renounce the difficult yet noble task of improving the lot of man in his totality, and of all people, with the excuse that the struggle is difficult and that constant effort is required, or simply because of the experience of defeat and the need to begin again, that person would be betraying the will of God the Creator."[10]

We are all called to free humanity of suffering. The pope reminds us that "part of the teaching and most ancient practice of the Church is her conviction that she is obliged by her vocation—she herself, her ministers and each of her members—to relieve the misery of suffering, both far and near..."[11]

Collaboration is essential. "The obligation to commit oneself to the development of peoples is not just an individual duty," states the pope.

> It is an imperative which obliges each man and woman, as well as societies and nations. In particular, it obliges the Catholic Church and other Churches and Ecclesial communities, with which we are completely willing to collaborate in this field. In this sense, just as we Catholics invite our Christian brethren to share in our initiatives, so do we declare that we are ready to collaborate in theirs....
>
> Collaboration in the development of the whole person and of every human being is in fact a duty of all to all, and must be shared by the four parts of the world: East and West, North and South...[12]

A notion closely related to collaboration and interdependence, which the pope introduces later, is solidarity. John Paul describes solidarity as "a firm and persevering determination to commit oneself to the common good; that is to say to the good of all and of each individual, because we are all really responsible for all." The pope also describes solidarity as "a commitment to the good of one's neighbor with the readiness, in the Gospel sense, to 'lose oneself' for the sake for the other instead of exploiting him, and to 'serve him' instead of oppressing him for one's own advantage."[13]

The earth's resources belong to all. The pope reminds us of this basic principle of Catholic social teaching. In the worlds of his encyclical, "the goods of creation are meant for all." He explains: "That which human industry produces through the processing of raw materials, with the contribution of work, must serve equally for the good of all."[14]

A related principle to which John Paul referred earlier, is "each people's equal right 'to be seated at the table of the common banquet.'"[15] The gifts of God's creation can be compared, indeed, to the banquet table of life. And part of our Christian task is to help all people find a way to secure a place at that banquet and enjoy a fair share of the earth's bountiful gifts, as envisioned by the creator in the Book of Genesis.[16]

Global solidarity is the solution. Viewing this on an international level, the pope asserts that

> the stronger and richer nations must have a sense of moral responsibility for the other [economically weaker] nations, so that a real international system may be established which will rest on the equality of all countries....
>
> Solidarity helps us to see the "other"—whether a person, people or nation—not just as some kind of instrument, with a work capacity and physical strength to be exploited at low cost and then discarded when no longer useful, but as our "neighbor," a "helper" (cf. Genesis 2:18-20) to be made a sharer, on par with ourselves, in the banquet of life to which all are equally invited by God.[17]

In this regard, the pope suggests that the international trade system needs reform. We single out for reflection just one of his comments on the issue: "The international trade system today frequently discriminates against the products of the young industries of the developing countries and discourages the producers of raw material."[18]

We now move closer to our times and take a quick look at Pope John Paul II's 1999 apostolic exhortation "The Church in America." Here he applies some of his thoughts on human development and liberation to the American hemisphere, that is, to North, South and Central America and the Caribbean.

His thoughts take a special turn to the phenomenon of globalization. *Globalization* refers to the process by which we are becoming one global community. The Internet and other forms of instant communication, and expanding international commerce, are drawing us rapidly into one global family

The term "economic globalization" can have either positive or negative implications, though the negative often seem to predominate.

In "The Church in America," the pope states, "There is an economic globalization which brings some positive consequences, such as efficiency and increased production," and such consequences can lead to "greater unity among peoples" and "better service to the human family," he admits.

> However, if globalization is ruled merely by the laws of the market applied to suit the powerful, the consequences cannot but be negative. These are, for example,... unemployment, ... the destruction of the environment and natural resources, the growing distance between the rich and the poor, unfair competition which puts the poor nations in a situation of ever-increasing poverty.[19]

The solution to this in our hemisphere, he points out, is solidarity and greater collaboration among the various American nations. "The Church in America is called...to promote greater integration between nations, thus helping to create an authentic globalized culture of solidarity." In so doing, he affirms, we can help reduce "the negative effects of globalization such as the domination of the powerful over the weak."[20]

To go back to an earlier image, care must be taken that no person, or group or nation is excluded from the banquet table of God's bounty—or is forced to stand at the margins of economic life. To conclude with the pope's own words, "The Church in America must incarnate in her pastoral initiatives the solidarity of the universal Church towards the poor and the outcast of every kind. Her attitude needs to be one of assistance, promotion, liberation and fraternal openness. The goal of the church is to ensure that no one is marginalized."[21]

For Reflection

- *When you think of helping a neighbor who is hurting do you think only of the neighbor next door? Or does your concern go out to the larger community, even to the whole human family on a global level?*

- *Besides prayer, what actions can you take to lift the burdens of the suffering both near and far?*

- *What does freedom mean for you? In what areas of life do you need to seek greater freedom? How can you help another to experience a new kind of freedom?*

Closing Prayer

God of love, Father, Son and Spirit, we believe that you are with us always leading us onward, as individuals and as your people, to our full liberation and development. Inspired by Saint Paul, we are confident of this, that the one who began a good work in us will continue to complete it until the day of Christ Jesus.[22] Amen.

Notes

[1] Jack Wintz, "The Pope in Cuba: A Call for Freedom," *St. Anthony Messenger*, April 1998, p. 28.

[2] "The Pope in Cuba," p. 28.

[3] "The Pope in Cuba," p. 33.

[4] "The Pope in Cuba," p. 34.

[5] Luke 4:18-19.

[6] Jack Wintz, "Chile: The Human Rights Nightmare and the Papal Visit," *St. Anthony Messenger*, July 1987, p. 34.

[7] John Paul II, Encyclical "On Social Concern" (*"Sollicitudo Rei Socialis"*), #10.

[8] "On Social Concern," #17.

[9] "On Social Concern," #26.

[10] "On Social Concern," #30.

[11] "On Social Concern," #31.

[12] "On Social Concern," #32.

[13] "On Social Concern," #38.

[14] "On Social Concern," #39.

[15] "On Social Concern," #33.

[16] Genesis 1:28-31.

[17] "On Social Concern," #39.

[18] "On Social Concern," #43.

[19] "On Social Concern," #20.

[20] "On Social Concern," #55.

[21] "On Social Concern," #58.

[22] See Philippians 1:6

DAY FIVE
The Test of Suffering

Coming Together in the Spirit

It is no secret that Karol Wojtyla, as a young man and even during the early years of his pontificate, was a picture of health, vigor and virility. As an athlete skilled in soccer, swimming, canoeing and skiing, he exhibited a great physical presence.

During his papal trip to the United States in 1979, he rode through Manhattan in the back of a limousine with an opening in the roof that allowed him to be visible to the crowd from the waist up. He was in excellent physical condition, waving to the crowds with just the right amount of drama as the vehicle moved slowly along. (This was before the 1981 assassination attempt in Rome and the days of the "popemobile," with its bulletproof glass protecting the pope.)

These are all reminders of John Paul's healthier days when he had all the physical stamina and charm any human could want. The pope did regain—for a time— his health and vigor after recuperating from the 1981 assassination attempt. In the early nineties, however, a series of health problems began to take their toll. In 1992, the pope had colon surgery, involving removal of a non-cancerous tumor. The next year he fell and dislocated a shoulder. In 1994, he suffered a broken femur in another fall. An appendectomy followed in 1996. During these

years, moreover, a Parkinson-like condition, if not the
disease itself, began to reveal its visible effects.

The point of these sobering details is to show that John
Paul, our retreat director, was clearly entering the part of
his life's journey marked by failing health and suffering.

Describing the Holy Father in the fall of 1998, Cardinal
Joseph Ratzinger stated: "The pain is written on his face.
His figure is bent, and he needs to support himself on his
pastoral staff. He leans on the cross, on the crucifix..."[1]

We are thus setting up the context for Retreat Session
Five "The Test of Suffering." Again, as in previous sessions,
our retreat director teaches us first by his lived example
and then through words and insights that shed light on the
subject at hand. Even the pope's "leaning on the cross"—
to use Cardinal Ratzinger's description—conveys a
message without words. John Paul would lean on Christ's
cross in more ways than one.

Opening Prayer

Oh God, giver of life and healer of hearts, when we
are faced with suffering or illness, help us to see such
challenges, not as times of disgrace, but rather as times
of grace and potential growth. Give us heroic faith and
power to imitate Jesus in our time of testing so that our
love may grow stronger and that we may grow closer to
you. Amen.

RETREAT SESSION FIVE

The January 1998 papal trip to Cuba posed an
enormous contrast to John Paul's United States visit in

1979. The pope's athletic stamina was gone. Now his gait was slow and at times shuffling, his speech was often slurred and his hand sometimes trembled.

But frankly, there was something beautiful and noble in the pope's witness. His courageous perseverance in carrying out his activities as pope, despite his physical afflictions, was a heart-lifting example for all of us. This was, perhaps, doubly true for all those people around the globe who were themselves bearing some cross or affliction. Many of us, faced with the same tests, would be tempted to shrink from public view, as if infirmity were an embarrassment or personal disgrace.

Not so our brother John Paul II! He refused to go into hiding as long as he could effectively fulfill his ministry as pope. He bore his infirmities as if they were badges of honor and opportunities for imitating the courage of the suffering Christ.

His humble, unpretentious and unembarrassed acceptance of suffering was a dramatic form of witness. The pope offered the world a wonderful model for responding with grace to the test of suffering and illness. As Cardinal Ratizinger observed, John Paul II helps us realize that "even age has a message, and suffering a dignity and a salvific force."[2]

While the pope was in Cuba, this anecdote was circulating. Someone asked the pope if it would be better if he retired. "After all, Holy Father," the questioner pointed out, "you have trouble walking and your hand trembles."

"Fortunately," the pope quipped, "I don't run the Church with my feet or my hands, but with my mind!"

We cannot be certain of the authenticity of the story, but it captures something of the pope's spirit—and his ability to respond to challenges with good humor.

Besides being a heroic witness in the face of suffering,

Pope John Paul II has often written inspiringly on the subject. In 1984, for example, he published the apostolic letter "On the Christian Meaning of Suffering." When confronted with suffering, most of us desperately seek answers to the question *why*? Why me? Why now? Why in this unexpected form?

The pope, in his letter, states that Christ does not really give us an answer to such questions, but rather a lived example. When we approach Christ with our questions about the reason for suffering, says the pope, we cannot help noticing that the one to whom we put the questions "is himself suffering and wishes *to answer...* from the Cross, *from the heart of his own suffering....*"

"Christ does not explain in the abstract the reasons for suffering," he points out, "but before all else he says: 'Follow me!' Come! Take part through your suffering in this work of saving the world.... Gradually, *as the individual takes up his cross*, spiritually uniting himself to the Cross of Christ, the salvific meaning of suffering is revealed before him."[3]

In 1993, Pope John Paul II instituted the Annual World Day of the Sick as a way to bring compassion and greater attention to the sufferings of humanity, as well as to the mystery of suffering itself. The event is held on February 11 each year on the feast of Our Lady of Lourdes. The pope explains that the Lourdes' "shrine at the foot of the Pyrenees has become a *temple of human suffering.*"[4]

In John Paul's message for the First Annual World Day of the Sick (1993), he offered these words of comfort to suffering people around the world: "Your sufferings, accepted and borne with unshakeable faith, when joined to those of Christ take on extraordinary value for the life of the Church and the good of humanity."[5]

He also suggested in the same message that suffering

can be transformed into something noble and good: "In the light of Christ's death and resurrection, illness no longer appears as an exclusively negative event," he said. "[R]ather, it is seen as...an opportunity 'to release love..., to transform the whole of human civilization into a civilization of love' (Apostolic Letter *Salvifici doloris*, n. 30)."[6]

We cannot really choose to have no pain in our lives, because pain in some form is inescapable. We have no choice about pain or suffering. Sooner or later everyone must face it. Even Jesus and his mother had to undergo pain.

Whether we bear it with love or not, however, is a different matter. We do have a real choice there. We are free to choose "the pain of loving" or "the pain of not loving," the latter being a pain that is empty and barren— a pain without any redeeming qualities. We know that Jesus and his mother and other heroic witnesses like John Paul have chosen the "pain of loving." That is, they undergo suffering for the love of God and of humanity, so their pain has rich meaning.

In 1999, Pope John Paul II published a "Letter to the Elderly." Just as we noted earlier that the pope has shown a special concern to the youth of the world, so now he shows a similar concern for elderly people, who also represent a very important segment of humanity. Like the pope himself, a good number of elderly people are susceptible to suffering and failing health.

In his comments to the elderly, the pope reveals some of his own sentiments about the challenges associated with aging, failing health and the end of life on earth. He encourages his elderly brothers and sisters "to live with serenity" the years that the Lord has granted to them.

Then, John Paul adds this poignant, personal note:

... I feel a spontaneous desire to share fully with you

my own feelings at this point of my life, after more
than twenty years of ministry on the throne of
Peter.... Despite the limitations brought on by age,
I continue to enjoy life. For this I thank the Lord. It
is wonderful to be able to give oneself to the very
end for the sake of the Kingdom of God!

At the same time, I find great peace in thinking
of the time when the Lord will call me: from life to
life! And so I often find myself saying, with no trace
of melancholy, a prayer recited by priests after the
celebration of the Eucharist: *In hora mortis meae voca
me, et iube me venire ad te*—at the hour of my death,
call me and bid me come to you. This is a prayer of
Christian hope, which in no way detracts from the
joy of the present, while entrusting the future to
God's gracious and loving care.

"Iube me venire ad te!": this is the deepest yearning
of the human heart, even in those who are not
conscious of it.[7]

John Paul concludes his "Letter to the Elderly" with a
prayer. His words and sentiments suggest that he will
pass "The Test of Suffering" with honors! This prayer,
composed by John Paul, makes a perfect ending for our
retreat session.

Grant, O Lord of life, that we may...savour every
season of our lives as a gift filled with promise for
the future.

Grant that we may lovingly accept your will, and
place ourselves each day in your merciful hands.

And, when the moment of our definitive
"passage" comes, grant that we may face it with
serenity, without regret for what we shall leave
behind. For in meeting you, after having sought you
for so long, we shall find once more every authentic
good which we have known here on earth, in the
company of all who have gone before us marked

with the sign of faith and hope.

Mary, Mother of pilgrim humanity, pray for us "now and at the hour of our death." Keep us ever close to Jesus, your beloved Son and our brother, the Lord of life and glory.

Amen.[8]

For Reflection

- *After years of good health and physical vigor, Pope John Paul II suffered a rather quick and depressing series of losses. What health problems have challenged you? Have you met the challenge with faith and perseverance?*

- *How does an example of suffering like that of John Paul II change your view of your own suffering?*

- *What is your understanding of redemptive suffering? If you knew that all the people in a hospital were bearing their suffering out of love for you and for the world, would you consider their "pain of loving" a very potent and redemptive force?*

Closing Prayer

Lord Jesus, you are a great model of suffering. You teach us that the best answer to the mystery of suffering is not really an answer or explanation so much as an example, namely, your own living example of bearing the pain of the cross out of love for God and for the world. Help us to follow your example of complete trust in your Father's love—and in his power to raise you up, as well as all his children, and to set the whole world free. Amen.

Notes

[1] Quoted in Jack Wintz, "The Witness of a Cross-Carrying Pope," *St. Anthony Messenger*, February 1999, p. 27.

[2] "The Witness of a Cross-Carrying Pope," p. 27.

[3] Pope John Paul II, "On the Christian Meaning of Suffering" (*"Salvifici doloris"*), #26.

[4] Pope John Paul II, "Message of the Holy Father Pope John Paul II for the First Annual World Day of the Sick," 1993, #6.

[5] "Message of the Holy Father Pope John Paul II for the First Annual World Day of the Sick," #5.

[6] "Message of the Holy Father Pope John Paul II for the First Annual World Day of the Sick," #3.

[7] Pope John Paul II, "Letter to the Elderly," #17-18.

[8] "Letter to the Elderly," #18.

DAY SIX
Forgiving and Asking Forgiveness

Coming Together in the Spirit

What would it be like to be the target of an assassin's bullet? We can only imagine that, besides the great physical pain, one would also be confronted with the emotional trauma of feeling hated, rejected and unjustly attacked— and of having one's precious right to life brutally violated.

We all know that Pope John Paul II came face to face with just such a violent assault in St. Peter's Square on May 13, 1981. As the pope was circling the square in an open car before a general audience, a young Turk, Mehmet Ali Agca, shot him in the stomach. Severely wounded, John Paul was rushed away to undergo a six-hour operation at Rome's Gemelli Hospital.

What were the pope's sentiments about his assailant? Four days later, on May 17, the pope left his bed for the first time to deliver a message from the hospital at the time of the Angelus. Among other things, he expressed his concern about others wounded in the assault and his thanks for the prayers of well-wishers. Regarding Mehmet Ali Agca, he said: "I pray for the brother who shot me and I have sincerely forgiven him."[1] The story was carried on the front page of newspapers around the world.

In all, the pope spent seventy-seven days in the

hospital recovering from his injuries. Two years later, another front-page story would report that the pope went to Rome's Rebibbia prison on December 27, 1983 and met with Ali Agca alone in his cell for twenty minutes.

After the meeting, the pope told reporters, "What we said to each other is a secret between him and me. I spoke to him as a brother whom I have forgiven and who enjoys my confidence."[2]

By his own living example, Pope John Paul II has shown us the beauty and the importance of forgiving those who have done evil or harm against us. In Retreat Session Six, we will explore further how the pope's act of forgiveness flows from the teachings of Christ in the gospel.

We will also take time to consider our need, as individuals and as Church, to ask pardon of God and of our neighbor for offenses committed against them. In this regard, we will look closely at the well-publicized Jubilee event known as the Day of Pardon, over which Pope John Paul II presided during Mass on the first Sunday of Lent, March 12, 2000. During this special Mass at St. Peter's Basilica in Rome, Pope John Paul II asked forgiveness for the Church's sins and errors committed during the last two millennia. More than once in his homily on the Day of Pardon, the pope announced: "Let us forgive and ask for forgiveness." This two-pronged approach to the theme of forgiveness is our subject for Day Six.

Opening Prayer

Christ Jesus, on this earth your love was so unfathomably rich that you forgave even your enemies, even those putting you to death. Help us to imitate you in showing others this kind of self-emptying love and mercy.

We also ask from you forgiveness for our sins, as well as the sins of our brothers and sisters throughout the world. You, our most caring God, are merciful and compassionate, slow to anger, perfectly loving and faithful. We ask that you accept our repentance and that of all your people. Forgive us as we forgive those who have sinned against us.

RETREAT SESSION SIX

There is a stronger connection than we might imagine between forgiving and asking for forgiveness. In the Our Father, we pray, "Forgive us our trespasses as we forgive those who trespass against us." In Matthew's Gospel, right after Jesus teaches this prayer to the people he adds, "For if you forgive others their trespasses, your heavenly Father will also forgive you; but if you do not forgive others, neither will your Father forgive your trespasses."[3]

There is a mysterious inner dynamic between our forgiving others and our being forgiven. Moreover, the cause-and-effect dynamic is immediate! It is not merely an if/then kind of thing in the sense that *if* we forgive people here and now, *then* God will forgive us in the hereafter. Future forgiveness in heaven is important, of course, but there is also a simultaneous effect in this dynamic. No sooner do I open my heart in forgiveness, than I perceive myself as forgivable, allowing me to forgive myself and accept God's forgiveness.

It is not only a theological truth, therefore. It is also a psychological truth. When I am able to make an act of self-giving love that sets another free, I know simultaneously that another loving being—our all-loving God or a loving neighbor—is also able to set me free in the same way.

This is part of the reason why John Paul II found it

theologically and psychologically meaningful to hold a Day of Pardon for the sins and mistakes of the Church. It is safe to assume that the pope has often forgiven his offenders. But, let's focus on his forgiveness of his would-be assassin, Mehmet Ali Agca. Just as the pope was able to humbly forgive him, so also could he know—in his bones, so to speak—that God could forgive him his sins, as well as those of other repentant Christians.

Jesus' Teaching on Forgiveness

There is no question that when John Paul II forgave his assassin—as well as when he decided to call a Day of Pardon for the whole Church—he was faithfully fulfilling the teaching of Jesus on forgiveness and reconciliation as found in the gospel.

A spirit of forgiving and asking forgiveness ranks very high among the sublime sentiments of Jesus in his Sermon on the Mount. "When you are offering your gift at the altar," he says, "if you remember that your brother or sister has something against you, leave your gift there before the altar and go; first be reconciled to your brother or sister, and then come and offer your gift."[4]

A few verses later, Jesus announces: "You have heard that it was said, 'An eye for an eye and a tooth for a tooth.' But I say to you, Do not resist an evildoer. But if anyone strikes you on the right cheek, turn the other also."[5]

"You have heard that it was said, 'You shall love your neighbor and hate your enemy.' But I say to you, Love your enemies, and pray for those who persecute you, so that you may be children of your Father in heaven, for he makes his sun rise on the evil and on the good, and sends rain on the righteous and unrighteous."[6]

In John's Gospel, after washing his disciples' feet, Jesus urges them to follow his "new commandment" of love: "As I have loved you, you also should love one another."[7] And, as we all know, Jesus loved us "to the end."[8] His mission was not to condemn imperfect human beings—to lock them in their sinful state—but to forgive and liberate them from sin. In Jesus' own words, "God did not send his son into the world to condemn the world, but in order that the world might be saved through him."[9]

When people commit offenses against us, we have the choice to forgive or not. If we refuse to forgive, we hold them—and ourselves—in a state of enmity or paralysis. Our relationships are frozen in place and cannot move forward. The same thing can happen between nations and religions, too. If we are to grow as individuals, as a Church and as a global human family, we need to accept and imitate Jesus' style of forgiving love.

The Day of Pardon

Pope John Paul II felt that the Jubilee year was a not-to-be-missed opportunity for the Catholic community to publicly confess its sins and failings. In order for the Church truly to move forward into a new millennium, the pope strongly believed that a cleansing of conscience had to happen first.

The pope's courageous decision to hold the Day of Pardon seemed to strike a sympathetic chord around the world. Some felt the pope did not go far enough but, in general, John Paul's leading the whole Church in a public act of repentance received a widely favorable response from both religious and secular quarters.

Under the headline of "Pope Asks Forgiveness for Errors of the Church Over 2,000 Years," *The New York Times* ran the following front-page story.

ROME, March 13—Saying "we humbly ask forgiveness," John Paul II today delivered the most sweeping papal apology ever, repenting for the errors of his Church over the last 2,000 years....

The public act of repentance, solemnly woven into the liturgy of Sunday Mass inside St. Peter's Basilica, was an unprecedented moment in the history of the Roman Catholic Church, one that the ailing 79-year-old pope pushed forward over the doubts of even many of his own cardinals and bishops. He has said repeatedly that the new evangelization he is calling for in the third millennium can take place only after what he has described as a "purification of memory"....

The pope also mentioned the persecution of Catholics by other faiths. "As we ask forgiveness from our sins, we also forgive the sins committed against us," he said.[10]

After his homily on the Day for Pardon, the Holy Father presided over a monumental prayer ceremony that was nothing less than a public apology for the sins of the Church.

The ceremony, identified bluntly as a "Confession of Sins and Asking for Forgiveness," was divided into seven categories[11]:

Confession of Sins in General. (Each of the seven categories was introduced by a representative of the Roman Curia with an opening prayer. This was followed by a short period of silence and then a solemn prayer by the pope.)

Confession of Sins Committed in the Service of the Truth. Included here were acts of violence and intolerance on the part of Christians in the service of the truth. The Holy Father asked God to forgive these offenses against tolerance and "the great commandment of love" and to "accept our resolve to seek and promote truth in the gentleness of charity."

Confession of Sins Which Have Harmed the Unity of the Body of Christ. Pardon was asked here for the division created among Christians and for sins that "rent the unity of the Body of Christ." The pope's prayer was that all Christians become reconciled and "experience anew the joy of full communion."

Confession of Sins Against the People of Israel. Here the pope acknowledged the many sins committed by Christians "against the people of the Covenant." John Paul II expressed repentance for such behavior and the wish that we "commit ourselves to genuine brotherhood with the people of the Covenant."

Confession of Sins Committed...Against...the Rights of People, and Respect for Cultures and Religions. The prayer was that Christians repent attitudes and behaviors of domination toward other religions and groups. The pope expressed sorrow for Christians who, through a "mentality of power [have] violated the rights of ethnic groups and peoples and shown contempt for their cultures and religious traditions."

Confession of Sins Against the Dignity of Women and the Unity of the Human Race. Repented under this category were offenses against human dignity and against "women, who are all too often humiliated and emarginated." The Holy Father asked pardon for those times when "the equality of [God's] sons and daughters has not been acknowledged, and Christians have been guilty of attitudes of rejection and exclusion, consenting to acts of discrimination."

Confession of Sins in Relation to the Fundamental Rights of the Person. This prayer included "minors who are victims of abuse, for the poor,...the unborn killed in their mother's womb...." John Paul II asked God's forgiveness for all those who show "contempt for the 'little ones' who are so dear to [God]."

Purifying Our Own Memories Today

On this day of our retreat, we look back at this historic act of public repentance not simply as a reminder of an important event of the Great Jubilee Year. Rather, we want to use the event as a reminder that right here, right now, we need to strike our own breasts in repentance for our failings and to approach Christ for the gift of forgiveness and reconciliation. Nor is our purpose simply to look back in judgment or disdain at those Church members of the past who failed in the categories listed above. We need instead to look at our own faults, realizing that we are all sinners in need of God's mercy.

Yes, on this next to last day of our retreat, we want to enter into the spirit of the Day of Pardon. We willingly undergo our own purification of memory and cleansing of conscience, so that we, too, can move ahead to a new day!

We open our hearts, therefore, to the good news proclaimed by the pope during his Day of Pardon homily: "Although Christ, the Holy One, was absolutely sinless, he agreed to take our sins upon himself. He agreed in order to redeem us; he agreed to hear our sins to fulfill the mission he received for the Father, who—as the evangelist John writes—'so loved the world that he gave his only Son, that whoever believes in him…may have eternal life' (Jn 3:16)."[12]

The image of Christ shedding his blood to wash away our sins is a helpful image to reflect upon as we personally search for forgiveness. As we know so well, Jesus does not return evil for evil, but instead, forgives with love. When nails were driven into Jesus' hands and a spear thrust into his heart, it was not vengeance and condemnation that flowed forth from his wounds. Rather it was a cleansing flood of forgiveness—the blood and water of Christ's self-emptying love for the sake of the world's salvation.

And if we turn to the Last Supper—and to the eucharistic celebrations of our own day—do we not see the same dramatic gesture of love? Jesus hands over his body to those gathered around the table. He also offers the cup of his blood, saying "Drink from it, all of you; for this is my blood of the covenant, which is poured out for many for the forgiveness of sins."[13]

For Reflection

- When have you resisted forgiving someone who injured you? How does this attitude affect your sense of your own "forgivability"?

- Is there something for which you first must forgive yourself, in order to sense God's forgiveness? Do you have the faith to believe that God can forgive any trespass?

- In light of Jesus' example and teachings, how do you rate yourself in terms of forgiving and asking forgiveness?

Closing Prayer

Lord Jesus, you are our model for forgiving others. You courageously lived your own teachings—doing good to those who hated you and blessing those who cursed you. Your love was so pure and high-minded that you sought only to build up and serve the life of your neighbor, no matter what harm was inflicted on you. Your style of forgiving revealed the purest face of love, for when you forgave, you sought no advantage for yourself, only your neighbor's highest good! Teach us this kind of self-giving love. Amen.

Notes

[1] *The New York Times*, May 18, 1981, pp. 1, 8.

[2] *The New York Times*, May 18, 1981, p. 1.

[3] Matthew 6:14-15.

[4] Matthew 5:23-24.

[5] Matthew 5:38-39.

[6] Matthew 5:43-45.

[7] John 13:34.

[8] John 13:1.

[9] John 3:17.

[10] Alessandra Stanley, " Pope Asks Forgiveness for Errors of the Church Over 2,000 Years," *The New York Times*, March 13, 2000.

[11] Condensed from the Homily of the Holy Father on the "Day of Pardon," Sunday, March 12, 2000.

[12] Homily of the Holy Father on the "Day of Pardon."

[13] Matthew 26:27-28.

DAY SEVEN
Back to Bethlehem

Coming Together in the Spirit

Our retreat with Pope John Paul II ends where it began—strongly centered on Christ. At the beginning of his papacy, John Paul urged the Christian faithful—gathered at St. Peter's Square in Rome and tuned in around the world—to fearlessly open the door to Christ. "Don't be afraid," he said, "to welcome Christ and accept his power."

The pope's entire pontificate was focused on Christ the Redeemer. A culminating point of his papacy, as the pope himself suggests, was his prayerful pilgrimage to the land of Jesus' birth during the great Jubilee—late March of the year 2000.

On March 22, at a welcome ceremony at Tel Aviv airport, Pope John Paul II said, "Today, it is with profound emotion that I set foot in the Land where God chose to 'pitch his tent.'"[1] It was a wonderful choice of words. The pope was affirming both God's presence among the people of the covenant as well as that incredible presence that started in Bethlehem 2000 years ago when "the Word became flesh and lived among us."[2]

On this our final day of retreat, the words and actions of John Paul II in the land of Jesus' birth will help us to reflect prayerfully on the meaning of Jesus' Incarnation.

"In this year of the two thousandth anniversary of the

Birth of Jesus Christ," the pope explained at the Tel Aviv Airport, "it has been my strong personal desire to come here and pray in the most important places which, from ancient times, have seen God's interventions....["][3] John Paul also spoke of the special opportunity and "privilege of visiting...places...closely connected with the Life, Death and Resurrection of Jesus Christ...."[4]

Opening Prayer

Lord Jesus, Word made flesh, it is a privilege to follow in your footsteps through the land you made your own—even if only by way of these pages. And to do this through the eyes and faith-filled words of Pope John Paul II is also an honor. Through your Holy Spirit, may this holy pilgrimage unite us more closely to you, who are at once our human brother and our God. Amen.

RETREAT SESSION SEVEN

Our primary aim today is to explore the mystery of Jesus' Incarnation and redemption of humanity. Although the pope visited many places and dealt with many issues during his pilgrimage to the Holy Land, our focus here is only on the Holy Father's visits to Bethlehem, Nazareth and the Church of the Holy Sepulcher in Jerusalem.

When the pope's helicopter landed in Bethlehem on March 22, the pope bent down and kissed a bowl of local soil. Because this familiar papal gesture has usually been reserved for sovereign nations, some observers wondered if the pope was overtly supporting Palestinian statehood. But the pope's spokesman, Joaquin Navarro-Valls, suggested that respect for the Incarnation was the real focus of the gesture. "It would be very strange," Navarro-Valls said, "if the Holy Father didn't kiss earth from the land where Jesus was born."

The pope's symbolic kiss reminds us further that, when God made the earth his home at the birth of Jesus, all land took on a new sacredness. The "land where Jesus was born" is really the whole earth—the whole universe—and has no political borders. Though Bethlehem and its surroundings were especially honored by the birth of Christ, the honor extends to the whole planet as well.

During his homily while celebrating Mass in Manger Square, Pope John Paul II shared these words:

> For two thousand years, generation after generation of Christians have pronounced the name of Bethlehem with deep emotion and joyful gratitude. Like the shepherds and the wise men, we too have come to find the Child, "wrapped in swaddling clothes and lying in a manger" (Lk 2:12). Like so many pilgrims before us, we kneel in wonder and adoration before the ineffable mystery which was accomplished here.[5]

Then the pope suggested that he saw his coming to Bethlehem in the year 2000 as the culmination of his papacy, and indeed of his whole faith journey. *"Bethlehem is the heart of my Jubilee pilgrimage.* The paths I have taken lead me to this place and to the mystery it proclaims."[6] It is as if he was born to lead us and all God's people back to Bethlehem to contemplate the meaning of the Incarnation.

As you may recall, on Day Two of this retreat we focused on the theme of "Prayer: Taking Time to Listen." We told the story of how the Holy Father, after celebrating Mass at Manger Square, visited the grotto of the Nativity and prayed in solitary silence for more than fifteen

minutes. The following three quotes taken from the
pope's homily at Bethlehem may serve as rich food for
some moments of silent contemplation at this point.

> At the dawn of the new millennium, we are called
> to see more clearly that time has meaning because
> here Eternity entered history and remains with us
> forever.[7]
>
> The silence and poverty of the birth in Bethlehem
> are one with the darkness and pain of the death
> of Calvary. The Crib and the Cross are the same
> mystery of redemptive love; the body which Mary
> laid in a manger is the same body offered up on the
> Cross.[8]
>
> In the cave of Bethlehem... "God's grace has been
> revealed" (*Titus* 2:11). In the Child who is born, the
> world has received "the mercy promised to our
> fathers, to Abraham and his descendants forever"
> (cf. *Lk* 1:54-55). Dazzled by the mystery of the
> Eternal Word made flesh, we leave all fear behind
> and we become like the angels, glorifying God who
> gives the world such gifts.[9]

The pope chose March 25, 2000, as the day to visit
Nazareth because it is the feast of the Annunciation, the
real starting point of the Incarnation. It commemorates
the sacred moment of Jesus' conception by the Holy
Spirit in the womb of Mary—the very first moment of
the Eternal Word's becoming flesh and entering human
history.

Of course, we do not know the exact date either of
Jesus' birth or conception. Once December 25 was chosen
by the Church as the date to celebrate the birth of Christ,
it was reasonable to commemorate his conception nine
months earlier on March 25.

John Paul II's homily during the Mass at the Basilica
of the Annunciation in Nazareth offers us a profound
reflection on the meaning of Jesus' Incarnation.

We are gathered to celebrate the great mystery
accomplished here two thousand years ago. The
Evangelist Luke situates the event clearly in time
and place: "In the sixth month, the angel Gabriel
was sent by God to a town in Galilee called
Nazareth, to a virgin betrothed to a man named
Joseph... The virgin's name was Mary."[10]

The specifying of time and place and the names of
real human beings, indeed, reminds us that this event,
initiated by God, is an intervention in actual human
history. And for us Christians, it is the focal point of
history itself!

But in order to understand what took place in
Nazareth two thousand years ago, we must
return to the Reading from the Letter to the
Hebrews. That text enables us, as it were, to listen
to a conversation between the Father and the Son
concerning God's purpose for all eternity. [The
Son is saying to the Father:] "You, who wanted no
sacrifice or oblation, prepared a body for me. You
took no pleasure in holocausts or sacrifices for sin."
Then I said, "God, here I am! I am coming to obey
your will" (10:5-7). The Letter to the Hebrews is
telling us that, in obedience to the Father's will, the
Eternal Word comes among us to offer the sacrifice
which surpasses all sacrifices offered under the
former Covenant. His is the eternal and perfect
sacrifice which redeems the world.[11]

The pope is making a close link between the mystery
of the Incarnation and the mystery of Christ's death
and resurrection. The divine Word's self-emptying love
manifested through the Incarnation is as total a sacrifice
as Jesus' self-giving death on the cross. We are reminded
of a comment of the late Scripture scholar Raymond
Brown. He noted "some theologians have so appreciated
the intensity of the love in the Incarnation that they have

wondered whether that alone might not have saved the world even if Jesus was never crucified."[12]

The pope's reflections also remind us that we no longer see God as demanding human sacrifice or animal sacrifices to atone for human sin. The end of human sacrifice came about when Abraham understood that the sacrifice of his son Isaac was not really what God wanted. And the perception that animal sacrifices were needed to appease an angry or vengeful God disappeared with the coming of Jesus. Now we understand more fully that what really saves and forgives us is God's total gift of self and willingness to love us at all costs, even at the cost of his own human life.

As we have seen, the mystery of the Incarnation is closely linked to the mystery of the death and resurrection of Jesus. Both are expressions of God's self-emptying love. The pope also points out that both the empty tomb and Golgotha, where Jesus was crucified, are housed in the Church of the Holy Sepulcher.

We reflect on a few short passages from John Paul's homily during Mass at the Church of the Holy Sepulcher, Sunday, March 25, 2000.

> The Resurrection of our Lord Jesus Christ is the sign that the Eternal Father is faithful to his promise and brings new life out of death: "the resurrection of the body and life everlasting." The mystery is clearly reflected in this ancient church...which contains both the empty tomb—the sign of the Resurrection—and Golgotha—the place of the Crucifixion. The good news of the Resurrection can never be separated from the mystery of the cross.[13]
>
> Here at the Holy Sepulcher and Golgotha, as we renew our profession of faith in the Risen Lord, can we doubt that in the power of the Spirit of Life we will be given the strength to overcome our divisions and to work together to build a future of

reconciliation, unity and peace? Here, as in no other place on earth, we hear the Lord say once again to his disciples: "Do not fear; I have overcome the world!" (cf. *Jn* 16:33)[14]

From this place, where the Resurrection was first made known to the women and then to the Apostles, I urge all the Church's members to renew their obedience to the Lord's command to take the Gospel to all the ends of the earth. At the dawn of a new Millennium, there is a great need to proclaim from the rooftops the Good News that "God so loved the world that he gave his only Son, that whoever believes in him should not perish, but have eternal life" (*Jn* 3:16).[15]

For Reflection

- *Consider how the life of Pope John Paul II was focused on Christ the Redeemer. Is your life centered on Christ? Is Christ your model? Your source of meaning, power and life?*

- *What is the meaning of the Incarnation for you? Do you sense its transformative power in the world you inhabit and in your own human nature? How do you bring Christ's presence into the world?*

- *To "be not afraid" is a matter of firmly believing that God walks with us, inviting us to rely totally on God's love and step forward through our fears. Which fears keep you from following God more closely? How can mindfulness of God's presence inspire you to overcome your fears?*

Closing Prayer

Gracious God, our deepest reason for courage is the revelation that a loving savior has come to live among us and to walk with us through our fears. Help us to embrace this good news and to open wide the door to Christ, who alone can show us how to overcome fearsome obstacles. Give us the wisdom to see that our greatest fear should be that of being separated from you and your saving love. Amen.

Notes

[1] Speech of the Holy Father, welcome ceremony in Israel, Tel Aviv Airport, Tel Aviv, Israel, March 21, 2000.

[2] John 1:14.

[3] Speech of the Holy Father, Tel Aviv Airport.

[4] Speech of the Holy Father, Tel Aviv Airport.

[5] Speech of the Holy Father, Manger Square, Bethlehem, Israel, March 22, 2000.

[6] Speech of the Holy Father, Manger Square.

[7] Speech of the Holy Father, Manger Square.

[8] Speech of the Holy Father, Manger Square.

[9] Speech of the Holy Father, Manger Square.

[10] Homily of John Paul II at Mass in the Basilica of the Annuciation, Nazareth, Israel, March 25, 2000.

[11] Homily of John Paul II at Mass in the Basilica of the Annuciation.

[12] Raymond Brown, *A Retreat with John the Evangelist: That You May Have Life* (Cincinnati: St. Anthony Messenger Press, 1999), p. 24.

[13] Homily of the John Paul II at Mass in the Church of the Holy Sepulchre, Jerusalem, Israel, March 26, 2000.

[14] Homily of the John Paul II at Mass in the Church of the Holy Sepulchre.

[15] Homily of the John Paul II at Mass in the Church of the Holy Sepulchre.

Going Forth to Live the Theme

As we glance back at the life of Pope John Paul II, we see a bold human figure who comes across as "larger than life." And indeed, he is larger than life because he prayerfully tapped into a power that gives him strength beyond his own human resources.

John Paul hinted at this in Day Two of our retreat, "Prayer: Taking Time to Listen." He said that prayer, which is communication with God, always involves two participants, God and ourselves. And the one with the greater influence, he reminds us, is God. It is vital, therefore, that we open ourselves to this source of power and let God's love work in us.

John Paul II's familiar motto, "Do not be afraid to open the door to Christ," should remain with us. We should make this theme our own as we go forth from this retreat.

When we open wide the door to Christ, we have two options. We can welcome Christ to cross over the threshold into our space or we can pass over the threshold into Christ's realm. As a matter of psychology, we tend to favor the first choice. Our first instinct is to invite Christ to come into our space, our dwelling. To most of us, that option seems safer. It is our turf, so to speak, and we feel more in control there.

A familiar passage in the Book of Revelation suggests just that option. The risen Jesus says, "Behold, I stand at the door and knock. If anyone hears my voice and opens the door, I will enter his house and dine with him and he with me."[1] This is a comforting image of the soul's union with Christ. Jesus comes into our hearts, embraces us and strengthens us in our unique identity. It is an affirming and healing experience. And, perhaps, it prepares us for the second option.

The second option—crossing the threshold and venturing into Christ's space and reality—seems more daring, even frightening. We feel less in control as we move into the mysterious space of the risen Christ, whom not even the universe can contain.

But if we have allowed Christ to come into our humble space and have come to know his gentle love and healing concern, we are given the courage to cross the threshold into his great love. Yes, we leave our defenses behind and cross over into Christ's presence and all-consuming love. But being with Christ is a safe place to be. Christ's intentions toward us are not to harm or diminish us in any way. On the contrary, he wants to nurture us and lead us into wholeness and into the "glory of God," which Saint Irenaeus says is the human person fully alive.

"Do not be afraid," Jesus tells us. "Let yourself be open to my transforming love and power. You will not lose your identity. Rather you will blossom into your truest self—into the full stature of Christ. In so doing you will find your true meaning and definition and happiness."

As John Paul II has said in *Redemptor Hominis*, "In Christ and through Christ we have come to acquire full awareness of our dignity, of the heights to which we are raised, of the surpassing worth of our humanity, and of the meaning of our existence."[2] Do not be afraid to cross the threshold into Christ. Christ is our most sublime destiny!

Notes

[1] Revelation 3:20-21.

[2] Adapted from *Redemptor Hominis,* #11.

Deepening Your Acquaintance

Bernstein, Carl and Marco Politi. *His Holiness: John Paul II and the Hidden History of Our Time*. New York: Doubleday, 1996.

Kupczak, Jaroslaw. *Destined for Liberty: The Human Person in the Philosophy of Karol Wojtyla/John Paul II*. Washington: Catholic University of America Press, 2000.

O'Brien, Darcy. *The Hidden Pope: The Untold Story of a Lifelong Friendship That Is Changing the Relationship Between Catholics and Jews: The Personal Journey of John Paul II and Jerzy Kluger*. New York: Daybreak, 1998.

Weigel, George. *Witness to Hope: The Biography of Pope John Paul II*. New York: Cliff Street Books, 1999.

Wojtyla, Karol (Pope John Paul II). *Crossing the Threshold of Hope*. New York: Knopf, 1995.

———. *The Collected Poems of Karol Wojtyla/The Place Within*, translated by Jerry Peterkiewicz. New York: Random House, Inc., 1982.

———. *Love and Responsibility*. New York: Farrar, Straus & Giroux, 1981.

———. *The Pope Speaks to the American Church: John Paul's Homilies, Speeches, and Letters to Catholics in America*. San Francisco: HarperSanFrancisco, 1992.

————. *The Theology of the Body According to John Paul II: Human Love in the Divine Plan.* Boston: Daughters of St. Paul, 1997.

———— and Joseph G. Donders. *John Paul II: The Encyclicals in Everyday Language.* Maryknoll, N.Y.: Orbis, 2001.

———— et alia. *An Invitation to Joy: Selections from the Writings and Speeches of His Holiness John Paul II.* New York: Simon & Schuster, 1999.